**Sen**
Bible _ _ _ _ _ _ _ _ _ _

Give Thanks with a Grateful Heart (Book 1)
7 Studies for Individuals or Groups on "Being Thankful"

Senior Saints Ministry

Equipping Seniors and Senior Ministries

 Give thanks to the LORD, for He is good;
His love endures forever. Psalm 107:1

Senior Saints Ministry

Equipping Seniors and Senior Ministries

A Division of:

Fruitful Minis-Trees

ISBN-13: 978-1480114647

ISBN-10: 1480114642

 Give thanks to the LORD, for He is good;
His love endures forever.   Psalm 107:1

Senior Saints
Bible Study Series

Give Thanks *with a Grateful Heart* (Book 1)
7 Studies for Individuals or Groups on "Being Thankful"

Introduction

"Pray without ceasing; in everything **give thanks**;

for this is the will of God in Christ Jesus for you."

1 Thessalonians 5:17-19

The purpose of this study guide is to encourage

one another to **Give Thanks** (*with a Grateful*

Heart). We thank you for your consideration of

using this as your study guide.

Give thanks to the LORD, for He is good;
His love endures forever.　　*Psalm 107:1*

We hope and pray that it will lead you into a deeper relationship with our Lord and Savior, Jesus Christ, in which you have a grateful heart, giving thanks to Him.

Our hope is that this study guide will be easy enough for all to use and encouraging enough that all (whether "seasoned senior saints", or those who have just come to trust in Jesus as their Savior) will benefit from it.

Following this introduction is a section titled "Suggestions for Use". There you will find various suggestions on how individuals and leaders can best use this guide.

May the Lord bless you.

 Give thanks to the LORD, for He is good; His love endures forever.   Psalm 107:1

Senior Saints Ministry

Equipping Seniors and Senior Ministries

We hope that you will consider our ministry for further discipleship material. The purpose of our ministry is to encourage one another (especially the "Seasoned Saint") to *"go therefore and make disciples"* (Matthew 28:19). Our ministry resources consist of:

 † "Senior Saints" and "Go! Make Disciples": Study Guides

 † Music: Inspirational, Traditional, Devotional

 † Gifts for yourself and for your loved ones

 † Lifestyle helps for Seniors

Please visit us at: www.SeniorSaints.net

 Give thanks to the LORD, for He is good; His love endures forever.   Psalm 107:1

You may contact us at:

Karl and Tammy Graham

Phone us Toll Free at: 888-998-0507

Email: Karl@SeniorSaints.net or

Tammy@SeniorSaints.net

Give thanks to the LORD, for He is good;
His love endures forever.   Psalm 107:1

Contents:

Introduction   1

Suggestions for Use of this Study Guide   7

✝ Study 1   "Receive Christ, Overflow with
Thankfulness"   13

✝ Study 2   "Be at Peace ... and be Thankful   19

✝ Study 3   "Thankful that I Didn't Do That"   23

✝ Study 4   "Be Watchful and Thankful"   27

✝ Study 5   "Give Thanks"   31

✝ Study 6   "Don't Worry ~ Be THANKFUL!"   35

✝ Study 7   "Speaking of Thanksgiving"   39

Group Contact Information   45

Give thanks to the LORD, for He is good;
His love endures forever.   *Psalm 107:1*

"Study to show thyself approved unto God,

a workman that need not to be ashamed,

rightly dividing the Word of Truth."

2 Timothy 2:15

 Give thanks to the LORD, for He is good;
His love endures forever.   Psalm 107:1

Suggestions for Use of this Study Guide

➢ These study guides are designed for either individual or group use. Any size group will be able to benefit from the questions. Jesus taught in Matthew 18:20 "For where two or three gather in my name, there am I with them."

➢ We are also reminded of the 12 apostles whom Jesus discipled. Accordingly, a group of 12 or so seems to bring about good fellowship with one another.

Give thanks to the LORD, for He is good; His love endures forever.   Psalm 107:1

➢ Though the questions in these study guides often seem simple and easy, we hope and pray that they will help you to seriously consider the answer you give for each question.

➢ If meeting as a group, a group "leader" or "host" would be beneficial.

➢ While each study has its own Bible passage inserted on the page, it would be valuable for participants to bring their own Bibles along. Having extra Bibles on hand, provided by the host, is often appreciated. Try to keep some extra pens and pencils available as well.

Give thanks to the LORD, for He is good; His love endures forever.   Psalm 107:1

> ➢ A good host will *"Practice hospitality"* *Romans 12:13.* We suggest that the host provide food and beverages for participants. Often times others will feel more involved in the group if they are asked to bring something as well (cookies, brownies, cupcakes, beverages, etc.).

> ➢ The Host / Leader should prepare for this "gathering time of fellowship". Usually an hour to an hour and a half is a good amount of time to allot for the gathering.

> ➢ Allowing 10-15 minutes of social fellowship prior to promptly beginning the study gives participants a chance to, well, fellowship together!

 Give thanks to the LORD, for He is good; His love endures forever.   Psalm 107:1

➢ Opening the time together in prayer, asking the Lord to lead and guide your study, is a great way to begin.

➢ Each study will begin with a Bible passage. In a group setting, we would encourage you to read this passage out loud, perhaps together, in unison.

➢ If any of the questions seem to be "personal", perhaps even "intrusive" for a participant in a group setting, or if anyone in the group feels uncomfortable answering a particular question, we would encourage the rest of the group to respect their desire to refrain from answering.

Give Thanks   *Give thanks to the LORD, for He is good;*
His love endures forever.   *Psalm 107:1*

➢ We encourage everyone to participate. Leaders are encouraged to ask specific individuals what they think and how they feel about particular questions.

➢ Try your best to avoid "tangents," and having only a few participants dominate the conversation.

➢ We encourage each member of the group to have his or her own study guide to take home and read prior to gathering together.

➢ There is space after each question for your thoughts and answers to be written.

 Give thanks to the LORD, for He is good; His love endures forever. Psalm 107:1

> ➢ At the end of the study guide there is a handy page for you to write group members contact information. This will allow you to keep in touch with one another throughout the study.

> ➢ May the Lord bless you as you and / or your group embark on this study of *Giving Thanks with a Grateful Heart*.

~ Study 1 ~

"Receive Christ,
Overflow with Thankfulness"

Suggested "Group Study" Format

Start Time: _____

- ➤ Fellowship for 15 minutes

- ➤ Gather, greet, pray

- ➤ *Ask "What is something you are thankful*
    for this week?"

- ➤ Read the verse of the week

- ➤ Discuss questions

- ➤ Share prayer requests

- ➤ Pray

 Give thanks to the LORD, for He is good;
His love endures forever.   Psalm 107:1

Verse of The Week: Colossians 2:6-8

"So then, just as you received Christ Jesus as Lord, continue to live in Him, rooted and built up in Him, strengthened in the faith as you were taught, and **overflowing with thankfulness.**"

Questions:

1. Have you received Christ Jesus as your Lord?

2. How do you know that you have received Christ Jesus as Lord?

Give thanks to the LORD, for He is good; His love endures forever.   Psalm 107:1

3. What does it mean to be "rooted", "built up" and "strengthened" in the faith?

4. Who were some of the people in your life who have taught you about Christ Jesus?

5. What have you taught others about the Lord?

 Give thanks to the LORD, for He is good; His love endures forever.   *Psalm 107:1*

6. How do you live in Him on a day to day basis?

7. Are you a "thankful" person?

8. Do others see you as a thankful person?

9. Are you "overflowing with thankfulness"?

Give thanks to the LORD, for He is good; His love endures forever.   Psalm 107:1

Prayer Requests

- Remember to ask about these prayer requests next week!

-

-

-

-

Pray and fellowship:

"They devoted themselves to ... fellowship ... and to prayer. " (Acts 2:42)

 Give thanks to the LORD, for He is good; His love endures forever.   Psalm 107:1

"Study to show thyself approved unto God,

a workman that need not to be ashamed,

rightly dividing the Word of Truth."

2 Timothy 2:15

~ Study 2 ~

"Be at Peace ... and be Thankful"

Suggested "Group Study" Format

Start Time: _____

- ➢ Fellowship for 15 minutes

- ➢ Gather, greet, pray

- ➢ *Ask "What is something you are thankful for this week?"*

- ➢ Read the verse of the week

- ➢ Ask questions

- ➢ Share prayer requests

- ➢ Pray

Give thanks to the LORD, for He is good;
His love endures forever.   Psalm 107:1

<u>Verse of The Week:</u>   Colossians 3:15

"Let the peace of Christ rule in your hearts, since as members of one body you were called to peace. And **be thankful**."

<u>Questions:</u>

1. What is the "peace of Christ"?

2. Is the "peace of Christ" a rule in your heart?

Give thanks to the LORD, for He is good; His love endures forever.   *Psalm 107:1*

3. Is God at peace with you?

4. How are peace and thankfulness related?

5. Are you thankful for something today?

6. Name 3 things you are thankful for:

Give thanks to the LORD, for He is good;
His love endures forever.   *Psalm 107:1*

Prayer Requests

- Remember to follow-up on last week's prayer requests!

-

-

-

-

Pray and fellowship:

They devoted themselves to ... fellowship ... and to prayer. (Acts 2:42)

Give thanks to the LORD, for He is good; His love endures forever. Psalm 107:1

~ Study 3 ~

"Thankful that I Didn't Do That"

Suggested "Group Study" Format

Start Time: _____

- ➤ Fellowship for 15 minutes

- ➤ Gather, greet, pray

- ➤ *Ask "What is something you are thankful for this week?"*

- ➤ Read the verse of the week

- ➤ Ask questions

- ➤ Share prayer requests

- ➤ Pray

Give thanks to the LORD, for He is good; His love endures forever.   Psalm 107:1

Verse of The Week: 1 Corinthians 1:14

"I am thankful that I did not baptize any of you except Crispus and Gaius"

Questions:

1. Are you thankful that you "<u>did not</u>" do something?

2. Why were you thankful for something you did not do?

3. Why was Paul thankful that he did not baptize someone, especially when baptism seems like a good thing to do?

4. Can you think of a time when it may have been better to not have done something, than to have done it and caused disunity?

5. Can you think of any other incidences in the Bible when someone did not do something?

Give thanks to the LORD, for He is good; His love endures forever. *Psalm 107:1*

6. Is there a time when you were thankful someone did "not do" something for you?

Prayer Requests

- Remember to follow-up on last week's prayer requests!

-

-

-

-

Pray and fellowship:

They devoted themselves to ... fellowship ... and to prayer. (Acts 2:42)

Give thanks to the LORD, for He is good; His love endures forever.   Psalm 107:1

~ Study 4 ~

"Be Watchful and Thankful"

Suggested "Group Study" Format

Start Time: _____

- ➢ Fellowship for 15 minutes

- ➢ Gather, greet, pray

- ➢ *Ask "What is something you are thankful for this week?"*

- ➢ Read the verse of the week

- ➢ Ask questions

- ➢ Share prayer requests

- ➢ Pray

Give thanks to the LORD, for He is good; His love endures forever.   Psalm 107:1

Verse of The Week: Colossians 4:2

"Devote yourselves to prayer, **being watchful and thankful."**

Questions:

1. What are you to be watchful for?

2. Who and what do you pray about?

Give Thanks *Give thanks to the LORD, for He is good; His love endures forever.   Psalm 107:1*

3. How do your prayers reflect thankfulness?

4. In what way can you be more "devoted" to prayer?

Give thanks to the LORD, for He is good;
His love endures forever.   Psalm 107:1

Prayer Requests

- Remember to follow-up on last week's prayer requests!

-

-

-

-

Pray and fellowship:

They devoted themselves to ... fellowship ... and to prayer. (Acts 2:42)

Give thanks to the LORD, for He is good; His love endures forever.   Psalm 107:1

~ Study 5 ~

"Give Thanks"

Suggested "Group Study" Format

Start Time: _____

- ➢ Fellowship for 15 minutes
- ➢ Gather, greet, pray
- ➢ *Ask "What is something you are thankful for this week?"*
- ➢ Read the verse of the week
- ➢ Ask questions
- ➢ Share prayer requests
- ➢ Pray

Give thanks to the LORD, for He is good; His love endures forever.   Psalm 107:1

Verse of The Week: Matthew 26:26

"While they were eating, Jesus took bread, and when **He had given thanks**, He broke it and gave it to His disciples, saying, "Take and eat; this is my body."

Questions:

1. Why would Jesus "give thanks" *while* they were eating?

2. What is a good reason to "say grace" during mealtime? What isn't?

3. Is there something in your life that is hard to be thankful for?

4. How can we express our thankfulness to Him?

Give thanks to the LORD, for He is good; His love endures forever.   *Psalm 107:1*

Prayer Requests

- Remember to follow-up on last week's prayer requests!

-

-

-

-

Pray and fellowship:

They devoted themselves to … fellowship … and to prayer. (Acts 2:42)

 Give thanks to the LORD, for He is good; His love endures forever.   Psalm 107:1

~ Study 6 ~

"Don't Worry ~ Be THANKFUL!"

Suggested "Group Study" Format

Start Time: _____

➢ Fellowship for 15 minutes

➢ Gather, greet, pray

➢ *Ask "What is something you are thankful for this week?"*

➢ Read the verse of the week

➢ Ask questions

➢ Share prayer requests

➢ Pray

 Give thanks to the LORD, for He is good; His love endures forever.   Psalm 107:1

Verse of The Week: Philippians 4:6

"Do not be anxious about anything, but in every situation, by prayer and petition, with **thanksgiving**, present your requests to God."

Questions:

1. What are some anxieties you have in your life?

2. In what situations might it be acceptable to God to be anxious?

Give thanks to the LORD, for He is good; His love endures forever.   Psalm 107:1

3. How do you handle the stresses in your life?

4. How can we best present our requests to Him?

5. Why is important to God that we present our requests to Him with Thanksgiving?

Give thanks to the LORD, for He is good; His love endures forever.   *Psalm 107:1*

Prayer Requests

- Remember to follow-up on last week's prayer requests!

-

-

-

-

Pray and fellowship:

They devoted themselves to ... fellowship ... and to prayer. (Acts 2:42)

Give thanks to the LORD, for He is good; His love endures forever.   Psalm 107:1

~ Study 7 ~

"Speaking of Thanksgiving"

Suggested "Group Study" Format

Start Time: _____

- ➢ Fellowship for 15 minutes

- ➢ Gather, greet, pray

- ➢ *Ask "What is something you are thankful for this week?"*

- ➢ Read the verse of the week

- ➢ Ask questions

- ➢ Share prayer requests

- ➢ Pray

Give thanks to the LORD, for He is good;
His love endures forever.   Psalm 107:1

Verse of The Week: 2 Corinthians 9:11

"You will be enriched in every way so that you can be generous on every occasion, and through us **your generosity will result in thanksgiving** to God."

Questions:

1. Are you a generous person?

2. What are some occasions where you were enriched by being generous?

Give thanks to the LORD, for He is good; His love endures forever.   Psalm 107:1

3. Do you see your generosity resulting in thanksgiving to God?

4. Are you more thankful towards the person (who was generous to you) or towards God?

5. How can you be more generous?

6. How can you be more thankful?

 Give thanks to the LORD, for He is good; His love endures forever. Psalm 107:1

Prayer Requests

- Remember to follow-up on last week's prayer requests!

-

-

-

-

Pray and fellowship:

They devoted themselves to ... fellowship ... and to prayer. (Acts 2:42)

Give thanks to the LORD, for He is good; His love endures forever.   Psalm 107:1

Senior Saints Ministry

Equipping Seniors and Senior Ministries

We hope that you will consider our ministry for further discipleship material. The purpose of our ministry is to encourage one another (especially the "Seasoned Saint") to "go therefore and make disciples" Matthew 28:19. Our ministry resources consist of:

 ✝ "Senior Saints" and "Go! Make Disciples": Study Guides

 ✝ Music: Inspirational, Traditional, Devotional

 ✝ Gifts for yourself and for your loved ones

 ✝ Lifestyle helps for seniors … and more!

Please visit us at: www.SeniorSaints.net

 Give thanks to the LORD, for He is good; His love endures forever.   Psalm 107:1

You may contact us at:

> Karl and Tammy Graham
>
> Phone us Toll Free at: 888-998-0507
>
> Email: Karl@SeniorSaints.net or
>
>   Tammy@SeniorSaints.net

Give thanks to the LORD, for He is good;
His love endures forever.   *Psalm 107:1*

Group Contact Information

(This is a good place to list participants
in your group for contact information)

Name   **Phone / Email**

Give thanks to the LORD, for He is good;
His love endures forever.   *Psalm 107:1*

Made in the
USA
Monee, IL

14716652R20028